ART NOUVEAU MANDALAS

COLORING BOOK

JOHN ALVES

DOVER PUBLICATIONS, INC.
MINEOLA, NEW YORK

This collection of thirty-one original illustrations brings together two favorite themes—mandalas and the Art Nouveau style. They all feature the hypnotic magnetism of circular mandala patterns as well as the distinctive curvilinear forms of Art Nouveau and its naturalistic motifs. Part of the *Creative Haven* series for the experienced colorist, the perforated pages also make displaying your finished artwork easy.

Copyright

Copyright © 2017 by Dover Publications, Inc.
All rights reserved.

Bibliographical Note

Art Nouveau Mandalas Coloring Book is a new work, first published by Dover Publications, Inc., in 2017.

International Standard Book Number

ISBN-13: 978-0-486-81890-0
ISBN-10: 0-486-81890-X

Manufactured in the United States by LSC Communications
81890X01   2017
www.doverpublications.com

.